Svalbard

the land with the cold coasts

This is a book for you who have been in Svalbard and would like to remember some of your fine experiences in the polar world, it is a book for you who are thinking of going there and would like to know what will meet you, or for you who will never go there, but would nonetheless like to experience one of the world's last, untouched wildernesses.

If you approach Svalbard by plane on a clear day, you get the impression that you are coming to the world's largest pile of stones. From the plane window, it seems as though God, after fulfilling His creation of Mother Earth, was left with a handful of stones He had been unable to find a place for. He chose to throw them away close to the North Pole, in the belief that no-one would come up here anyway.

God was mistaken.

DEAR DIARY

The plane is approaching Longyearbyen.
Through breaks in the clouds I catch glimpses
of greyish black, naked mountains with
grey-green glaciers. For the next year,
this icy wasteland is going to be my home ...

History

According to notes in Icelandic Annals dating from 1194, it was Vikings from the west who were the first to see the mountains that rose from the ice-covered ocean. They called the land Svalbardur – the cold coasts (or edges). Nowadays, however, scholars are arguing about whether it was Svalbard or Greenland these Icelanders saw. The discovery of Svalbard is therefore con-

sidered to be more reliably attributable to the Dutch explorer, Willem Barents, who found the archipelago in 1596. Because of the pointed shape of its peaks, he named the largest island Spitsbergen.

After Barents, several others discovered the island realm in the North. International whaling took place in the region from around 1600 to 1750. From

1700 to 1800, it was Russian pomors who left their mark on Spitsbergen with their hunting stations. Norwegian interests did not awaken before the beginning of the 19th century when hunters from Norway began spending winters there in some earnest.

A gold rush atmosphere arose following the discovery of coal deposits in Svalbard. The area was a no-man's-

adventurers from far and near to the North dreaming of great riches to be won. They came to Spitsbergen, hammered a stake with their name on it into the frozen ground, and proclaimed the area theirs. This gradually led to a need for legislation and regulations, but it was not until after the First World War that agreement was reached on a Svalbard Treaty.

Already in 1906, the American, John Munroe Longyear, established the first coal mining company in Adventdalen, and the settlement of Longyearbyen, or Longyear City as it was then called, was founded. In 1916, Store Norske Spitsbergen Kulkompani took over the mining activities. It is that company, with more than 200 employees, that is now responsible for Norwegian coal mining in Svalbard.

The Svalbard Treaty was signed in 1920, and 39 nations have now acceded to it. Norway was given sovereignty over Svalbard in 1925, but nationals from the countries that are parties to the treaty have equal rights regarding access to Svalbard and residence there.

Of the approximately 2300 people currently residing in Svalbard, about 1400 - 1500 are Norwegians. Norwegian

A Russian Orthodox cross bears silent witness to the pomors having lived in Svalbard.

currency is used, and all the communities are subject to Norwegian authority. The supreme authority lies with the Governor, who is responsible for ensuring that Norwegian rights and obligations are adhered to in accordance with the Svalbard Treaty.

However, foreign interests, chiefly in the form of international research, are strongly evident in the region.

The Russians have also had several mining communities in Svalbard over the years. Now, only the mine at Barentsburg is working.

▲ Beluga whales used to be landed here for processing.

Until a few years ago, coal was mined ▶ by men who lay in drifts which, in places, were no more than 50 cm high. Nowadays, modern equipment makes the work easier and more comfortable.

land. There were no legal statutes or regulations, nor any court of law to solve the conflicts that arose when rumours of coal deposits attracted

Location and climate

Staying inside the ship on a Svalbard cruise feels futile. There's so much to see.

The archipelago is situated between 74°- 81° N and 10°- 35° E and has an area of around 63,000 square kilometres, approximately 60 % of which is covered by ice. The six largest islands are Spitsbergen, Nordaustlandet (North-East Land), Barentsøya (Barents Island), Edgeøya (Edge Island), Bjørnøya (Bear Island) and Prins Karls Forland (Prince Charles Foreland). People who live in Svalbard can boast of belonging to the world's northernmost population – the next stop is the North Pole, only 1200 kilometres further north.

The archipelago is surrounded by the Barents Sea in the east, the Norwegian Sea in the south, the Greenland Sea in the west and the Arctic Ocean in the north. Thanks to the Gulf Stream, Svalbard has a tolerable climate, with average temperatures of minus 14 degrees centigrade in winter and plus 6 degrees centigrade in summer.

You haven't really experienced Svalbard before you've tried all five seasons. Yes, they talk of five seasons here: spring, summer, autumn, the polar night and the light winter.

Hiking is popular in summer, preferably with an experienced person as a guide.

JULY

It is still light, both day and night. Confusingly light. You are still unable to separate day from night. Your sleeping rhythm is upset, and it is not unusual to turn night into day and day into night.

The most beautiful time is undoubtedly the transition from the polar night to the light winter, although some would perhaps maintain that the archipelago is at its finest in summer, when it is bathed in the midnight sun. Indeed, it is a really magnificent sight when you can experience a flat-calm sea and ice-blue glaciers calving day and night, sending turquoise icebergs out to sail a mirror-like sea. When you can admire a lazy seal basking on an ice floe, and day and night pass into one. When the 170 different kinds of vascular plants that are found up here, clinging to their stony footholds, paint the landscape. When bright green cliffs become alive with nesting birds, some 30 species all told, and reindeer graze peacefully at the foot of mountainsides that resemble Egyptian sphinxes. There are grey screes and a colourful profusion of flowers side by side. There are ice-cold, blue hues beneath a warm, rose-coloured sky. Raw, unspoiled Nature that, nevertheless, embraces you and gains a place in your heart with her vulnerability and her pride.

The summer in Svalbard is brief, but exhilarating. It is considered to last from around 1st June to 31st August.

◄ Little auks.   ▲ Purple saxifrage.

A bearded seal enjoys the summer in Monacofjorden.

◄ The polar bear mostly lives in the drift ice.   ▲ Kittiwakes resting on an ice floe.

Grazing reindeer. They need to build up fat reserves to survive the food shortage in winter.

The autumn, September, October and November, forms the golden transition to the polar night. You enjoy Nature's deep orange hues, emphasised by the low sun which gilds the mountains, giving us the final colourful thrills before everything vanishes in a veil of blue, polar twilight. And then, from the middle of November, the blue has gone, too.

SEPTEMBER

It is still quite light in the evenings, even though the midnight sun lost its grip on 23rd August. But now the blades of grass on the ground are beginning to take on a deep orange shade, reminding you that it is autumn. The first powdering of snow can come at any time.

With a starry sky, moonlight and a fantastic display of the northern lights, Christmas illuminations are superfluous. God himself has arranged for the decorations. You can almost expect to see reindeer drawing Father Christmas on his sledge across the heavens, on their way from the North Pole.

The polar night has descended, and the blackness of night fixes its grip on animals and people, mountains and fjords. Only on clear days, with a starry sky that can take anyone's breath away, and at full moon, do the outlines of the mountains appear as beautiful, silver-white backdrops, reminding us of what is concealed in the darkness. Once in a while, on a starry day, or night, the northern lights cascade over the heavens. Arrows of pink and green light dart towards white mountains, bright bands wave like banners beneath the stars, suddenly plunging down towards you in dramatic lunges, before withdrawing teasingly in a troll-like, stirring dance providing lifelong memories for those fortunate enough to experience a display.

Even though the average temperature in winter is around minus 14 degrees centigrade, a strong wind generally ensures that the actual temperature felt on the skin is considerably lower. It is not unusual for the temperature to drop to 30 below, so just about anything can really be expected here. In 1986, minus 46.3 degrees was measured. The highest summer temperature measured recently was plus 21 degrees centigrade in 1979.

The weather changes rapidly. One moment it may be dead calm, the next the wind may reach storm force in gusts. There may be sunshine one hour and dense fog the next. A winter storm with so much snow blowing around that you have little chance of seeing anything, not even the neighbouring house only 20 metres away, may last anything from half-an-hour to a week.

The Svalbard climate is dry. The area is called an 'arctic desert' and receives only 200 - 300 mm of precipitation a year. Consequently, there is surprisingly little snow. The dry snow does not stick well to the frozen ground and frequent, strong winds blow it into drifts, first here, then there.

However, not only are there sudden changes in the weather, the light and the seasons also shift rapidly. In the transition from autumn to the dark period, and from dark to light, there is twenty minutes less – or more – daylight each day. Only five weeks pass from when the sun shows itself for the first time in Longyearbyen on 8th March until it shines all day and night and acquires the status of midnight sun.

JANUARY

The darkness has been black for three months. One day, I begin to sense a weak blue shade in the blackness. A blue shade that becomes a little stronger each day. The light is returning.

FEBRUARY

One day, the sky in the south is light and shimmering, and the white mountain peaks are starting to get a stroke of bright pink. The sharp edge between the rose-coloured light and the blue shadow is creeping steadily down the mountainside. A little further each day.

If you have managed to endure the long polar night, it is difficult to describe how it feels when you come out on a cold February day and discover that the darkness is no longer black. It has obtained a slight bluish tinge in the south. A bluish tinge that becomes more and more intense from day to day and bathes the surroundings in a beautiful, cobalt-blue light that utterly spellbinds you. In the wake of the blue night, slowly but surely, a turquoise firmament, growing ever lighter, creeps over the crest of the mountain until finally you can see the first rose-coloured glow on the horizon, and then you know that the polar night is over for this time. The light is on its way back.

This is undoubtedly the most beautiful and most fascinating season. The light winter that follows, through March and April, does not lag far behind as regards beauty. It is then you experience the fantastic light which artists from every corner of the world try to capture with their camera, or brush and palette. The blackness of night is replaced by delicate pastel colours.

Beauty comes from within ...
In Svalbard, you are spellbound by the beauty both inside and outside the magnificent glaciers.

Settlements

Longyearbyen

The 'capital' of Svalbard, Longyear-byen, is situated in Adventfjorden, named after the British whaler "Adventure" which was operating there in 1656. Right up to the beginning of the 1990s, it was mainly coal mining that dominated and provided the livelihood of this small settlement, to some extent hunting, too, which had also left its mark on Svalbard as a whole over the previous century.

Nowadays, we meet a modern society with the same sophisticated lifestyle that can be found in any town on the mainland. A metropolis on a micro scale. The houses are simple, a mixture of two-storied prefabricated homes and rows of small, undetached houses. One of the first things that strikes a visitor to Longyearbyen is that sewers and water mains are located above ground level, resting on supports and insulated against the cold. This is because the permafrost makes it difficult to dig up the ground.

MARCH

We are living in a watercolour. On cloudless days, the world around us is painted in a soft range of colours from bright pink to deep turquoise, soft yellow, orange, blue and white. Longyearbyen is starting to wake up again...

The average age is low in Longyearbyen. There are many families with small children.

In Longyearbyen, you meet a young, modern society with lots of children and teenagers, but few old people. The settlement is not permanent – there are no natives in Svalbard. Everyone lives there for a limited period, depending on their job or assignment. The town which, during the heyday of the mining and the invasion of the hunters, was a typical male society, is now a family society. It has a primary school, a secondary school and a sixth-form college, and since 1993 even university education is given in Longyearbyen. Now, some 250 students and graduates from 22 nations are taking the University Courses in Svalbard (UNIS), studying arctic biology, arctic geology, arctic geophysics and arctic technology.

To live in Svalbard does not mean you have to forsake the good life. With sixteen shops, including a Body Shop, you have no need to journey to the mainland to shop. There are two hairdressing salons, a library, a church, a museum and an art gallery. A modern swimming pool built to international standards, a training studio and a sports hall make it simple to keep yourself fit. A choir, a folk dancing group, a football team and a wide variety of societies ensure that the inhabitants have plenty to do. The church functions as a sort of seamen's church, a social meeting place, and the town has a modern hospital.

To avoid the permafrost, sewers and water mains are placed above the ground.

You lack nothing, except when the plane bringing goods from the mainland is unable to land due to bad weather, or has insufficient space for freight because it is full of tourists. Then there may not be much to choose between in the shops.

Svalbard is a tax-free zone, so tobacco, alcohol and other wares that are liable to excise duty are cheaper than on the mainland. Some goods, however, are dearer because of the air freight costs.

Steeply roofed houses add colour and variety to the settlement. Mainly families with children live there; they need more space than the barrack-like houses can offer.

One reason why the average age of the town's population is low is that Longyearbyen has about 250 university students.

If you are expecting a small, primitive mining community where everyone knows everyone else, you will definitely be disappointed. Longyearbyen is a metropolis – a melting pot – with around 1500 people packed together between silent mountains bearing names like Sukkertoppen (Sugar Peak), Sarkofag (the Sarcophagus), Platåberget (Plateau Mountain) and Hiortfjellet (Stag Mountain). The Longyearbreen and Larsbreen glaciers lie like ice-cold reminders that the icy wasteland is not far away, even if it is a sophisticated lifestyle that dominates this tiny metropolis on the valley floor.

But sophisticated or not, the town undoubtedly has its peculiarities...

Perhaps you wonder why so many women in the town have short hair? Then you can try to imagine what their hair would look like after being hidden beneath a close-fitting cap or a scooter helmet most of the year. The "scooter cut" is widespread among the women in Longyearbyen, and the two hair-dressing salons always have enough to keep their scissors busy with!

Coal dust and sand stick to your shoes when you walk around outside, so it is normal to remove your shoes before you enter a house in Svalbard. This also applies to several public offices, shops and overnight accommodation premises. Some supply slippers. So remember not to have holes in your socks when you travel to Svalbard.

The residents do not use umbrellas when it rains. Umbrellas and handbags are never used by Svalbard residents. Only tourists carry them.

Ny-Ålesund

Ny-Ålesund is situated north-west of Longyearbyen, at the head of Kongs-fjorden, with the Kongsbreen glacier and the three peaks – Dana, Svea and Nora – as a magnificent backdrop. Here, too, it was coal mining that gave birth to the settlement, but following the King's Bay disaster in 1963, no mining has taken place here. Ny-Ålesund is now an international research centre with between 40 and 100 inhabitants from several countries.

The world's northernmost railway is in Ny-Ålesund, but it is no longer in running order.

The bust of Roald Amundsen in Ny-Ålesund is a favourite attraction for tourists and guides visiting the settlement.

Ny-Ålesund was also the starting point for Roald Amundsen's flight with the airship "Norge". On 11th May 1926, he set out on his journey over the still unknown part of the Arctic, via the North Pole, to land at Teller in Alaska 72 hours later. The mooring mast still stands as a monument to his flight.

Colliers in Barentsburg. These tough fellows don't see much daylight! ▲

Svea

Svea was actually owned by Swedish interests until 1934 when Store Norske Spitsbergen Kulkompani bought the area. Today it is Svea that holds the hopes of future mining in Svalbard alive. The new Central Field is still being investigated and the result will be presented in 2001. The miners work week-long shifts and travel by plane to and from Longyearbyen since there are no road links between any of the settlements on the island. The 45 kilometres of roads are mainly in and around Longyearbyen.

Hornsund is a research centre where eight Poles live all year round. It is situated about 250 kilometres from Longyearbyen and can only be reached by boat or helicopter, or by snow scooter in winter.

Barentsburg

Barentsburg is the last remaining Russian coal mining community on the islands. The Russians used to have mines at Pyramiden and Grumant, too, with hundreds of inhabitants, but both these communities are now ghost towns with empty buildings. Barentsburg, however, still has around 900 inhabitants. The Russians there live collectively, without any form of private housekeeping. All their meals are eaten in a large canteen, and their wages are paid at home in Russia on the day they return home again. Even though the post office is Norwegian and the currency used is Norwegian crowns, you get a real feeling of being in Russia.

The Russians try to be as far as possible self-sufficient. They have barns and greenhouses to supply meat, milk and vegetables. The Russians reckon

▲ The Russians sell home-made souvenirs in Barentsburg.

Following 'perestroyka', monuments of ► Lenin have been removed from many Russian towns. But they still stand in Barentsburg and Pyramiden.

they only have coal reserves for another 25 years. Their mining is not particularly profitable, and it is not unlikely that the Russian community, like the Norwegian, will concentrate more on tourism in future.

NOVEMBER

The polar night has set in.
Now it is dark all the time.
At full moon, the landscape is
bathed in a white, silvery light
reminding us of the fantastic
scenery surrounding us.
But when it becomes overcast,
the darkness is just as intense.

Mining

The quay for shipping coal is still operating in Longyearbyen.

Coal mining began in Svalbard almost 100 years ago, and is still the principal livelihood here. When John M. Longyear started mining here in 1906, he established at the same time the first settlement in the valley which also bears his name. His sale of the plant and settlement brought about the formation of the Store Norske Spitsbergen Kulkompani enterprise in 1916. As many as seven mines have operated around Longyearbyen. Some have been worked out, others have closed following tragic accidents. Twenty-six people died in an explosion in Mine 1 in 1920. The coal was still smouldering 22 years later.

Nowadays, only Mine 7 is being worked, but not with a view to export. It is only intended to supply coal to the power station in Longyearbyen.

◀ The "Father Christmas Mine". Lights shine from the windows of the old buildings at the abandoned Mine 2 throughout the dark period. At Christmas, an illuminated Christmas tree stands outside. The children in Longyearbyen "know" that Father Christmas lives here...

▼ The old-time "black gold".

Tourism

Tourism is now the second largest industry in Svalbard. As soon as the ice breaks up and the fjord becomes navigable, cruise ships show up, an annual sign that summer is just around the corner.

As our holiday habits gradually change, and more and more people choose adventure holidays instead of sunning themselves on a beach, the need also arises to experience more extreme parts of the world. Many of those who seek extreme tourism find their way to Svalbard. Here you can experience a different kind of holiday, whatever time of year you choose. Svalbard is a popular place for tourists from many countries, especially Germany, Sweden, Britain, France and Italy. Many visit on cruise ships, others arrive by plane. There are daily, scheduled flights from Tromsø.

APRIL

Spring tourism is at its height. Long convoys of snow scooters leave Longyearbyen every day, speeding out into the white countryside.

▲ Aboard the cruise ships, there's a celebration when latitude 80° N is crossed.

▲▲ Enjoying life. The snow scooter is a favourite means of transport.

If you come to Svalbard in summer, there are plenty of exciting offers to choose between. Day trips by boat can take you to Barentsburg, the Esmark glacier, Kapp Linné and Isfjord Radio Station, or to beautiful Tempelfjorden with the Tuna and von Postbre glaciers and the abandoned Russian settlement of Pyramiden. If you want to spend several days on a trip you have the chance to cross the 80° N parallel with one of the tourist boats that sail two or three times a week. Weather permitting, some sail as far north as Moffen, a large walrus colony. The walrus is totally protected and the population now numbers just over 2000.

A kayak or rubber dinghy can take you into small and large fjords to see icebergs drifting away after calving from a glacier. The turquoise colours of the glaciers are deep and intense. To witness the calving of a glacier, when large and small chunks of ice break off the snout, is like being in the midst of a war zone. First, there is an intense rattling, like machine guns in an ambush, as the ice fractures. Then the canons thunder as the block of ice loosens and crashes into the sea with a roar. It is best to be at a good distance then. The surface of the sea rises in protest as the iceberg strikes the water, a struggle takes place beneath the surface, accompanied by foaming froth and whirling currents, before everything settles down, and Nature is just as silent and secretive as she was a moment ago.

Svalbard can also offer exciting trekking trips, walks on glaciers and sightseeing by plane over the glaciers. If you are interested in fossils, you should join a rubber dinghy safari to Carolinedalen, an area famed for its abundance of fossils.

For those who are not dependent on travelling by sea over open water, spring is perhaps the most exciting time to visit Svalbard. From 19th April, the midnight sun shines over the archipelago. There is usually still enough snow for you to be able to get out on snow scooter trips, although those who prefer the silence should choose a trip with a dog sledge, perhaps the ideal way of experiencing the scenery and silence of Svalbard. Nevertheless, snow scooter trips are the most common ways of getting around. The snow scooter has become part of the culture in the areas surrounding the settlements on Spitsbergen. In Longyearbyen alone, there are almost as many snow scooters as people, around 1300 are registered. The various tour operators hire out both scooters, equipment, warm clothing and guides.

If you are not an adventurer who enjoys raising your adrenaline production by challenging Nature and testing your own endurance, there are enough thrills to experience in and around Longyearbyen itself.

In summer, the silence is broken by ▶ calving glaciers and the continuous humming of motor-powered cameras and video cameras.

Rubber dinghies land tourists from the cruise ships.

Svalbard Museum.

mark the victims of a rampant influenza epidemic, said to have originated in Spain, that hit the population in 1918. Scientists in 1997 tried to open a few of the graves in search of the virus that took the lives of 1500 Norwegians. The scientists managed to find some living tissue, which they sampled. But they found that the corpses lay no more than 30 centimetres beneath the surface, probably not deep enough for the permafrost to have preserved them.

From the graveyard, you continue to the legendary, pink building called "Huset". This was built in 1951 and has served as hospital, school, post office, café and party premises, and church. It was vital, and sometimes difficult, to

If you are staying in the town, a visit to the museum is a must. It presents the history of hunting and mining in Svalbard, and is housed in the oldest building in town, once the barn for the cows that were imported to the islands.

If you walk from the museum to "Huset", you will pass a graveyard filled with white, wooden crosses. These

Nowadays, burials no longer take place in Svalbard, but urns carrying cremated ashes can still be laid to rest here. However, the graves of those who died in the influenza epidemic in 1918 are preserved.

▲ "Huset" is a natural meeting place in Longyearbyen. It houses a cinema and concert hall, a kiosk, a café, a gourmet restaurant with the world's northernmost wine cellar, a pub, a nightclub and a disco.

◄ "Kroa" is another, newer, popular venue.

You can also spend the night out-of-doors if you wish.

get all the partygoers on a Saturday night out of the building before the minister entered the pulpit the following morning! Nowadays, it houses the combined cinema and theatre, a kiosk, a restaurant, a café, a pub and a nightclub with a disco at the weekends. This is a natural meeting place with traditions. You've not been to Longyearbyen if you've not been in "Huset".

Just above there, in Nybyen (the new town), which was where the workers once had their communal living quarters, is Galleri Svalbard, the northernmost art gallery in the world. One of the attractions it offers is a permanent exhibition of works by the Norwegian painter, Kåre Tveter.

The town has three hotels. Two are built in a traditional, more or less international style. However, at Basecamp Spitsbergen, you can stay in a room designed as a replica of a hunter's shack, with rustic details like long underpants used as window curtains (they are new!)

You can also spend the night outside, either in an igloo or a tent. But if you intend leaving Longyearbyen remember that a gun and a guide are required.

Galleri Svalbard, boasting many, varied exhibitions, is much visited, also by the residents.

Arctic fauna

This is the kingdom of the polar bear. Man is a guest here. The polar bear is one of the world's largest predators and although it is a terrestrial mammal it lives most of its life in the sea and on the drift ice. However, it roams a great deal. When it is travelling over the archipelago, it happens each year that the polar bear encounters people. On such occasions, it is vital to be aware that you must pay this arctic king the respect he deserves. It is forbidden to hunt or frighten the polar bear. It is completely protected and may only be killed in self-defence. The bear moves unbelievably fast, as quickly as 60 kilometres an hour, though only over short stretches because it easily becomes overheated.

The bear is inquisitive, but also aggressive. Hunger can drive it to attack. So you must not rely on this big bear just being playful!

The polar bear loves food, and is certainly not stupid. It has an excellent sense of smell, and has often broken into a hut where it has smelt food and helped itself to the stores in the kitchen cupboard. Usually it gets in by removing the planks around a window or door, breaking in just like a common thief. It is generally most interested in the kitchen, where the food is kept, and opens tins by squeezing them between its paws. Packets of soup are opened with a gentle claw ...

Tracks! The bear can't be far away!

Male and female bears differ considerably in size. The male usually measures 2.2-2.5 metres from its nose to the tip of its tail, while the female normally measures 1.8-2.1 metres. Polar bears vary in weight during the year. In spring, a female weighs around 200 kg, whereas large males can weigh up to double that figure. The largest polar bear weighed in Svalbard scaled at 700 kg!

Polar bears feed chiefly on seals and need at least one seal a week to survive.

Perhaps one of the world's most photographed road signs! "Applies throughout Svalbard"! Should be taken seriously.

The chubby reindeer which graze peacefully both in the centre of Longyearbyen and out in the countryside are more frugal. You often wonder what food they are finding where they are scraping with their forehoofs in the solidly frozen ground, with or without a cover of snow.

Other mammals that can be seen include the arctic fox and the sibling vole, the latter having arrived with ships. There are also six species of seal. From a boat on a warm summer day, you can see seals basking on ice floes out on the fjord. If you are lucky you may also spot a beluga whale, or other whales, playing in the sea.

The arctic fox shifts its coat, becoming completely white in winter.

OCTOBER

The snow has settled on the mountains. The reindeer are scraping the frozen ground trying to find a few blades of grass and a little frozen lichen they can eat. We are approaching a more peaceful season.

◄ Walrus.   ▲ The Svalbard reindeer is smaller and stockier than its relative on the mainland.

Arctic tern poised for attack.

Thirty different species of birds have been found nesting in Svalbard in the summer. Only the Svalbard ptarmigan spends the winter on land here. The arctic tern is a beautiful bird and a typical migrant. It nests early in the summer and guards its nest with tooth and nail.

The Svalbard ptarmigan is so tame you can almost pick it up.

The arctic skua protects its eggs, but does not attack lower than the highest point.

◄ Communal living.   ▲ The little auk is a funny little bird with an infectious "laugh".

"The different child"

The Svalbard poppy - delicate and beautiful.

So, welcome to wonderland – the polar land. A realm of contrasts. A colourful society, not just for adventurers and hard people, but also for those who simply want to see, experience and get closer to themselves and Nature. And not least, for those who want to take photographs!

Svalbard is beautiful and largely untouched. Occasionally cold and arrogant, Nature here does not embrace you with instant warmth. It takes some time to penetrate beneath the uppermost layer of permafrost and get to know this proud and noble creation. Then you are captured by the mystical and vulnerable beauty of the islands. Svalbard does something to you. It is said that people are never the same after a visit here.

The archipelago up here in the North, in common with the more luxuriant valleys and rolling fields on the mainland, is also a child of Mother Norway. But it has not been equally liberally endowed with benefits in the shape of warmth and luxuriance. In this respect, Svalbard is Mother Norway's "different child". And it is frequently the case that, as a member of a family with a child that is different, you develop a very special relationship with that child. Meet Svalbard and judge for yourself...

DEAR DIARY

It is beyond me to imagine that I once looked upon Svalbard as a grey, barren, pile of stones. How can I have felt repugnance for anything so beautiful and soothing? My dislike has turned to love.

Large parts of Svalbard are legally pro-tected. The areas where you may travel freely, without reporting to the Governor first or applying for permission, are limited.

However, even when you are travel-ling in the open areas, there are rules you should follow.

Common sense rules for Svalbard

1. Don't be an arctic litterbug! Leave no lasting signs of your visit.

2. Birds and animals are not to be dis-turbed. Remember, you are the guest.

3. Help take care of the biodiversity. Do not pick flowers.

4. Leave old cultural remains alone. The law protects all traces of people from before 1946.

5. Pursuing, attracting or enticing polar bears is strictly prohibited. They are dangerous animals, but also vulnerable.

6. Do not leave the settlements without a suitable gun, and experience in using it.

7. Be considerate of others.

8. Contact the Governor's office (Syssel-mannen) if planning a longer field excursion. A mandatory registration applies for travel to large parts of Svalbard.

9. Acquaint yourself with the rules and regulations pertaining to travel and other tourist activities on Svalbard.

10. For the sake of both the environment and yourself, we recommend organ-ised tours.

© Egmont Bøker Fredhøi AS – SFG
N - 0055 Oslo
Tel: +47 22 47 11 50, Fax: +47 22 47 11 74
E-mail: sfg@egmont.no
www.touristbooks.com

Author: Ellinor Rafaelsen
Picture editor: Bård Løken
Editor: Trude Solheim
Design: Sissel Holt Boniface
Translation: Richard Binns
Prepress: Capella Media, Norway
Printed by: Nørhaven A/S, Denmark

ISBN 82-04-06947-2

Svalbard

POLHAVET

Sjuøyane
Phippsøya
Martensøya
Parrøya
Karl XII-øya
Kræmer-
pynten
Kvitøya
Hornodden
Nordkapp
Nordenskiöld-
bukta
Kapp Platen
Repøyane
Platen-
halvøya
Kapp Leigh Smith
Andrèeneset
Snøtoppen
Laponia-
halvøya
Prins
Oscars
Land
Leighbreen
Storøya
Italiaodden
Norskebanken
Lågøya
Botnia-
halvøya
Sverdrup-
isen
Orvin Land
Isispynten
Langgrunn-
odden
Storstein-
halvøya
Gustav V
Land
Nordaustlandet
Austfonna
Verlegenhuken
Moffen
Vestfonna
Hartogbukta
Isodden
Nordvestøyane
Velkomstpynten
Mosselbukta
Gotha-
halvøya
Bragebreen
Gustav Adolf
Land
Sørdomen
Klerckbukta
Amsterdamøya
Danskøya
Reinsdyr-
flya
Gråhuken
Scania-
halvøya
Svarknausflya
Haakon VII
Land
Valhallfonna
Lomfjord-
halvøya
Wahlberg-
øya
Vibebukta
Bråsvellbreen
Abeløya
Magdalenefjorden
Hornemantoppen
Albert I Land
Andrée
Land
Ny
Friesland
Sjubredrenna
Kong Karls Land
Breibukta
Kongsøya
Mitraa-
halvøya
Dovrefjell
Perriertoppen
Wilhelmøya
Bastianøyane
Rivalensundet
Kapp Mitra
Newton-
toppen
Svenskøya
Ny-Ålesund
Rørasfjellet
Kvitbreen
Kapp Payer
Kapp Hammerfest
Fuglehuken
Brægger-
halvøya
Engels-
bukta
James I
Land
SPITSBERGEN
Olav V
Land
Hannbreen
Sonklarbreen
Olgastretet
Prins
Grampian-
fjella
Dickson
Land
Pyramiden
Nordenskiöld-
breen
Einhyrningbukta
Kapp Ziehen
Karls
Oscar II
Land
Nord-
fjorden
Bünsow
Land
Negribreen
Grimfiela
Barents-
jøkulen
Schweinfurth-
berget
Barentsøya
Forland
Sassenfjorden
Sabine
Land
Wichebukta
Kapp Heuglin
Protektorfjellet
Longyearbyen
Adventdalen
Dunèrbukta
Freemansundet
Salpynten
Daudmannsodden
Coles
bukta
Helle-
fonna
Kapp Lee
Bläfjorden
Stonepynten
Isfjord-renna
Kapp Linné
Barentsburg
Skolten
Agardhbukta
Diskobukta
Gottexfjellet
Stonebreen
Ryke Yseøyane
Isfjord Radio
Nordenskiöld-
kysten
Nordenskiöld
Land
Gustav
fjellet
Sveagruva
Edgeøy-
jøkulen
Edgeøya
Isfjordbanken
Marvågen
Heer
Land
Russebukta
Diger-
fonna
Kong Johans Bre
Bellsund fyr
Akseløya
Fagerstafjella
Bellsund
Nathorst Land
Kvalpynten
Tjuvfjorden
Halvmåneøya
Kapp Lyell
Boltodden
Kvalvågen
Negerpynten
Dunderbukta
Berzeliustinden
Wedel
Jarlsberg
Land
Torell
Land
Storfjorden
Tusen-
øyane
Storvika
Beisaren
Hornbreen
Hambergbukta
Hornsundbanken
Hornsund
Hornsundtind
Sørkapp
Land
Isbukta
Hopen
Hornsundneset
Olsok-
bresen
Storfjordbanken
Hopen Radio
Stormbukta
Sørkappbanken
Kapp Thor
Sørkappøya
Sørkapp

Kvitøyjøkulen

Erik Eriksenstretet

Målestokk 1: 2 200 000
Ekvidistanse 300 m

| 0 | 25 km | 50 | 75 | 100 |

Kartgrunnlag fra Statens kartverk,
MOT 11060R94818

Captions for full-page illustrations:
Side 2:   Grønsteinfjellet in Isfjorden
Side 4:   Polar bear
Side 10: Blomstrandfjellet
Side 22: A dog team on the Eidembreen glacier
Side 26: Autumn at Isfjorden
Side 34: An ice cave on the east coast
Side 48: Dog sledging - perhaps the most
            beautiful way of experiencing Svalbard
Side 52: The Bråsvellbreen glacier
Side 68: Rain over the pack ice
Side 70: A swimming polar bear

PICTURE CREDITS:

Top = A
Top left = B
Top right = C
Bottom = D
Bottom left = E
Bottom right = F
Centre = G
Centre left = H
Centre right = I

Samfoto:
Trym Ivar Bergsmo: 15 D, 21, 38 D, 42 D, 51 EF
Ole F. Backer: 13 D
Per Eide: 4, 17 D, 34, 56 A
Pål Hermansen: 14 A, 17 A, 18, 19 A, 30, 36, 47, 57, 59 A, 63
Arne Strømme: 54 D, 56 D
Jørn Areklett Omre: 28, 45 A, 46
Øystein Søbye: 44
Asgeir Helgestad: 48 A, 59 D
Kristin Forsberg: 24
Ole B. Frøshaug: 48, 50 A, 55 H
Helge Sunde: 12, 40 A
Birger Areklett: 38 G

Knutsen:
Wilse: 41 B
Kjærnet: 42 A, 54 G

Tony Stone:
Schafer & Hill: 1
Pål Hermansen: 7, 39, 70
John Beatty: 68

Jan-Petter Lahall: 6, 8, 14 D, 19 D, 41 C, 45 D, 52, 60 DA, 61, 62

Villmarksfoto: 2, 9, 20, 22, 26, 60 G

Terje Rakke: 32, 33, 38 A, 40 D, 72

Jørn Henriksen: 13 A

Jan Töve: 10, 16, 43 BC, 50 D, 58, 64, 66

Ellinor Rafaelsen: 55 G

Gunny Sandblåst: 31

Camera/Nils Lund: 54 A

John W. Olsen: 55 D